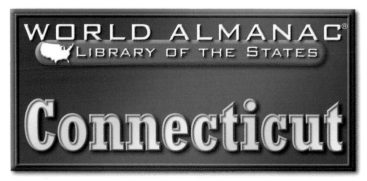

THE CONSTITUTION STATE

by Darice Bailer

Curriculum Consultant: Jean Craven,
Director of Instructional Support,
Albuquerque, NM, Public Schools

WORLD ALMANAC® LIBRARY

Please visit our web site at: www.worldalmanaclibrary.com
For a free color catalog describing World Almanac® Library's
list of high-quality books and multimedia programs, call
1-800-848-2928 (USA) or 1-800-387-3178 (Canada).
World Almanac® Library's fax: (414) 332-3567.

Library of Congress Cataloging-in-Publication Data

Bailer, Darice.
    Connecticut, the Constitution State / by Darice Bailer.
        p. cm. — (World Almanac Library of the states)
    Includes bibliographical references and index.
    ISBN 0-8368-5131-5 (lib. bdg.)
    ISBN 0-8368-5301-6 (softcover)
    1. Connecticut—Juvenile literature. I. Title. II. Series.
    F94.3.B28   2002
    974.6—dc21   2002022700

This edition first published in 2002 by
World Almanac® Library
330 West Olive Street, Suite 100
Milwaukee, WI 53212 USA

This edition © 2002 by World Almanac® Library.

Design and Editorial: Bill SMITH STUDIO Inc.
Editor: Kristen Behrens
Assistant Editor: Megan Elias
Art Director: Jay Jaffe
Photo Research: Sean Livingstone
World Almanac® Library Project Editor: Patricia Lantier
World Almanac® Library Editors: Monica Rausch, Mark J. Sachner, Jim Mezzanotte
World Almanac® Library Production: Scott M. Krall, Tammy Gruenewald,
  Katherine A. Goedheer

Photo credits: pp. 4-5 © James L. Amos/CORBIS; p. 6 (left) © Painet, (right) © Corbis Royalty
Free; p. 7 (left) © PhotoDisc, (right) © Corel; pp. 8-9 © Corel; p. 10 © Bettmann/CORBIS; p. 11
courtesy of the Mohegan Tribal Museum Authority; p. 12 © Corel; p. 13 © Library of Congress;
p. 14 © Library of Congress; p. 15 © TimePix; p. 17 © Peter Stackpole/TimePix; p. 18 © Richard
Cummins/CORBIS; p. 19 © Diana Walker/TimePix; p. 20 (left to right) © Christie Silver,
© PhotoDisc, © Corel; p. 21 (left to right) © ArtToday, © Corel, © Corel; p. 23 © David
Muench/CORBIS; p. 26 (top) © PhotoSpin, (bottom) © PhotoDisc; p. 27 courtesy of Mystic CVB;
p. 29 © Corbis; p. 31 (all) © Library of Congress; p. 32 © Corel; p. 33 © ArtToday; p. 34 (top)
courtesy of Mystic CVB, (inset) © Corel; p. 35 © Damian Strohmeyer/TimePix; p. 36 courtesy of
Mystic CVB; p. 37 (all) © Library of Congress; p. 38 © PhotoDisc; p. 39 © ArtToday; p. 40
© ArtToday; p. 41 (all) © Dover; pp. 42-43 © Library of Congress; p. 44 (left) © PhotoDisc, (right)
© Artville; p. 45 (left) © PhotoDisc, (right) © Bob Gregson

Printed in the United States of America

2 3 4 5 6 7 8 9 07 06 05 04 03

Connecticut

Yankee Doodle Dandies

In 1636, Reverend Thomas Hooker left his church in the Massachusetts Bay Colony for what is today Connecticut. Unhappy with church leadership in Massachusetts, Hooker preached that "the foundation of authority is laid in the free consent of the people."

Hooker's words guided Connecticut citizens and lawmakers. Those words were the basis of Connecticut's Fundamental Orders: the first constitution in the American colonies and the first to declare that government rested on the consent of its citizens. The writers of the U.S. Constitution used similar ideas. Hooker became known as "the father of Connecticut," and Connecticut's official nickname became "the Constitution State."

Although Connecticut is the third-smallest of the fifty United States, it played a big role in the American Revolution, and in later years it continued to supply soldiers, ammunition, airplanes, submarines, and helicopters for the country's battles throughout the world. During the French and Indian War, Connecticut soldiers inspired a British physician to write the satiric "Yankee Doodle." In spite of the fact that the song was written to mock American soldiers, it nevertheless became a beloved patriotic song.

Just as Connecticut soldiers made an anthem out of mockery, so Connecticut settlers found opportunity in a land of rocky soil. The state has nurtured presidents George H. W. Bush and George W. Bush to lead the nation and such writers as Mark Twain and Harriet Beecher Stowe. The state has also reared inspiring heroes, including Nathan Hale and Prudence Crandall. Connecticut inventors Eli Whitney, Samuel Colt, and Samuel Morse helped make the world we know today.

▶ Map of Connecticut showing the interstate highway system, as well as major cities and waterways.

▼ The Sheffield Island Lighthouse was built in 1826 and replaced with the current lighthouse in 1868. It has not been used since 1902.

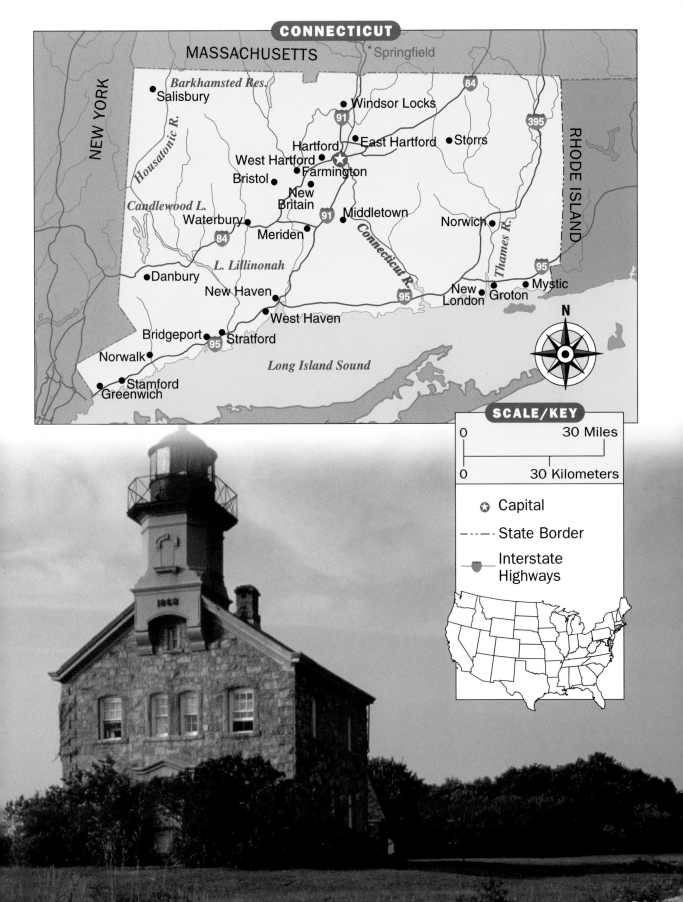

MASSACHUSETTS

Springfield

NEW YORK

Barkhamsted Res.

Salisbury

84

Windsor Locks

91

Housatonic R.

Hartford

East Hartford

Storrs

395

West Hartford

Farmington

Bristol

New
Britain

91

Middletown

Candlewood L.

Waterbury

84

Meriden

Norwich

Thames R.

RHODE ISLAND

L. Lillinonah

Connecticut R.

95

Danbury

New Haven

West Haven

95

New
London

Groton

Mystic

Bridgeport

95

Stratford

Norwalk

Stamford
Greenwich

Long Island Sound

N

SCALE/KEY

0   30 Miles

0   30 Kilometers

⭐ Capital

State Border

Interstate
Highways

Fast Facts

CONNECTICUT (CT), The Constitution State, The Nutmeg State

Entered Union

January 9, 1788 (5th state)

Capital	Population
Hartford	121,578

Total Population (2000)

3,405,565 (29th most populous state) — *Between 1990 and 2000 the state's population increased 3.6 percent.*

Largest Cities	Population
Bridgeport	139,529
New Haven	123,626
Hartford	121,578
Stamford	117,083
Waterbury	107,271

Land Area

4,845 square miles (12,548 square kilometers) (48th largest state)

State Motto

"Qui Transtulit Sustinet" — *Latin for* "He Who Transplanted Still Sustains"

State Song

"Yankee Doodle" *by Richard Shuckburgh, adopted in 1978*

State Bird

American robin — *Connecticut colonists adored this bird with its cheerful song because it reminded them of the European robin.*

State Animal

Sperm whale — *The sperm whale is the largest toothed whale and has the biggest brain of any animal.*

State Insect

European praying mantis — *The name* mantis *comes from the Greek word for "prophet." When this six-legged insect raises its two forelegs, it looks as if it is praying.*

State Tree

White oak

State Flower

Mountain laurel — *This woody shrub was originally called "spoonwood" because Native Americans and colonists made spoons and pipes out of its wood.*

State Shellfish

Eastern oyster

State Mineral

Garnet — *Connecticut is a world-supplier of this red gemstone.*

State Fossil

Eubrontes giganteus — *This is the footprint of a dinosaur that lived in Connecticut 200 million years ago.*

Barnum Museum, *Bridgeport*
Phineas Taylor Barnum of Bridgeport advertised his Grand Traveling Museum, Menagerie, Caravan, and Circus as "The Greatest Show on Earth." The Barnum Museum houses many of Barnum's treasures.

Putnam Memorial State Park, *Redding*
During the harsh winter of 1778–1779, about 3,100 men in the Connecticut militia spent the season freezing at an encampment now referred to as "Connecticut's Valley Forge." The site includes a museum, an interpretive trail, and an archaeological dig in progress.

Yale University, *New Haven*
Yale, the nation's third-oldest university, produced the nation's first doctor in 1729. The university offers visitors magnificent architecture, art museums, and theaters.

For other places and events, see p. 44.

BIGGEST, BEST, AND MOST

- The *Hartford Courant*, the first issue of which was printed in 1764, is the nation's oldest newspaper still being published today.

STATE FIRSTS

- **1828** Noah Webster of West Hartford published the *American Dictionary of the English Language*, creating a national standard for spelling, pronunciation, meaning, and usage.

- **1842** The Wadsworth Atheneum Museum of Art in Hartford opened as the nation's first free public art museum.

- **1939** Igor Ivan Sikorsky made the first successful helicopter flight at Stratford.

Yankee Doodle

In 1755, during the French and Indian War, British colonel Thomas Fitch of Norwalk gathered his troops to help fight the French. Legend has it that Fitch's sister, Betty, looked at the poorly dressed militia and raced off to a chicken coop. She scooped up some feathers and told the soldiers to wear them in their hats. A British physician named Richard Shuckburgh supposedly laughed when he saw the ragged soldiers walk by with feathers in their caps and invented new lyrics for a traditional European tune, creating "Yankee Doodle." A *doodle* was a dope or a fool, and British soldiers delighted in singing the song. Later, during the Revolutionary War, they sang it to insult the colonial soldiers. The Yankees, however, had the last laugh. Colonial soldiers sang the song throughout the war — perhaps most loudly while the British surrendered after the decisive battle at Yorktown, shortly before the Revolutionary War ended and the colonies gained their independence.

The official Connecticut version, according to the *Connecticut State Register and Manual* (2001):

Yankee Doodle went to town,
Riding on a pony,
Stuck a feather in his hat,
And called it macaroni.
Yankee Doodle keep it up,
Yankee Doodle dandy,
Mind the music and the step,
And with the folks be handy.

The Constitution State

> The warm, very warm heart of 'New England at its best,' such a vast abounding arcadia of mountains, broad vales and great rivers and large lakes and white villages embowered in prodigious elms and maples. It is extraordinarily graceful and idyllic.
>
> — Henry James, Sr., Intellectual (1811-1882)

As many as eight thousand years ago, humans reached what is now the state of Connecticut, probably after having crossed the North American continent in search of good hunting grounds. They built round houses in the central Connecticut River Valley and on the southern coast. In the valley, these settlers had plenty of flat, rich soil in which to grow corn, beans, squash, pumpkins, and tobacco. They could catch fish in the river, and those who lived along the coast also included oysters, clams, and lobster in their diet. Game, such as deer, wild turkey, bear, and moose, was plentiful in the Connecticut woods.

The Connecticut region eventually became home to the Algonquian-speaking peoples. These Native Americans called their land *Quinnehtukqut* — the "long river place," or "beside the long tidal river."

Several Algonquian-speaking groups lived in the region, and they did not always live in peace. The Pequots, whose name means "warrior" or "destroyer of people," were an aggressive and powerful force. They lived in the east and south, along the shore. In the 1600s Chief Uncas split off from the Pequots, leading a group that called themselves Mohegan. They settled near the Thames River, where they were often attacked by Mohawks from the north, who lived in the region that would become New York, and Pequots from the east.

The Coming of the Europeans

Captain Adriaen Block set off from New York Harbor in 1614 to explore New England. He was the first European to sail along the Connecticut shoreline and up the Connecticut

Native Americans of Connecticut
Hammonassett
Matabesec (Wappinger) Confederacy
Mohegan
Nehantic
Nipmunk
Paucatuck
Paugussett
Pequot (Mashantucket)
Podunk
Quinnipiac
Saukiog
Schaghticoke
Tunxis

River. Captain Block docked his ship near what would later become Hartford and traded with Native Americans for two weeks. He built a trading post there and then left. Because Block was Dutch, the Netherlands claimed ownership of Connecticut. The Dutch would eventually build a fort near present-day Hartford, but they did not establish a permanent settlement in Connecticut.

In April of 1631 a delegation of Algonquian sachems, or leaders, visited the pilgrims in Plymouth Colony and the Puritans in the Massachusetts Bay Colony. They told the colonists of their beautiful and fertile land. The sachems invited colonists to move to Quinnehtukqut, offering them eighty beaver skins a year and corn if they did. The offer may have been made because the Algonquians hoped the colonists would help them fight off other Native groups that were hostile to them.

Some colonists were interested. Although they had left England because of religious persecution, Puritan leaders in Massachusetts were not tolerant of people who disagreed with their political or religious beliefs. Puritan lawmakers enforced strict religious laws and did not allow dissent. In the Massachusetts Bay Colony, for instance, only church members could vote. Not all who lived in the Massachusetts Bay Colony were happy with this leadership. Some eventually broke off and set up their own communities.

▼ Settlers in New England started whaling as far back as the early 1600s. The *Charles W. Morgan*, now moored in Mystic, served longer than any whaler in history (1841–1921) and is the last of the wooden whaling ships.

The first non-Native settlement in Connecticut was established in 1633, when a group from Plymouth bought some land from Native peoples, built houses, and called their new home Windsor. The following year, in 1634, a separate group of Massachusetts colonists began living in what became known as Wethersfield.

The Native people helped the colonists survive in their new homes. Gifts of food during the cold winter of 1635 kept the colonists from starving to death. The Native Americans taught the English settlers how to plant and cook corn, weave mats and baskets, tan mink and beaver fur, and use native herbs for healing. For example, a remedy for coughing was to drink elm bark steeped in water. A number of these herbs and extracts are still used today.

In 1636, Thomas Hooker, a minister, decided to leave Massachusetts. Hooker believed that all men should have the right to vote, whether they were church members or not. He and a group of sixty colonists established Hartford — an area they named after Hertford, England.

That same year, the towns of Hartford, Windsor, and Wethersfield formed the Connecticut Colony. Hooker believed that lawmakers must serve their people. "The foundation of authority is laid, firstly, in the free consent of the people," Reverend Hooker said in a church sermon.

The Pequot Massacre

Relations between English settlers and local Pequots were not always good. The Pequots believed they had agreed to share the land with the settlers, while the settlers believed they had purchased the land outright. This created tensions between the two groups. In 1637, in revenge for an earlier skirmish, a Windsor man led ninety others on an early morning attack on a large Pequot village in West Mystic. The settlers set the village on fire, and between three hundred and seven hundred Pequots died in the blaze.

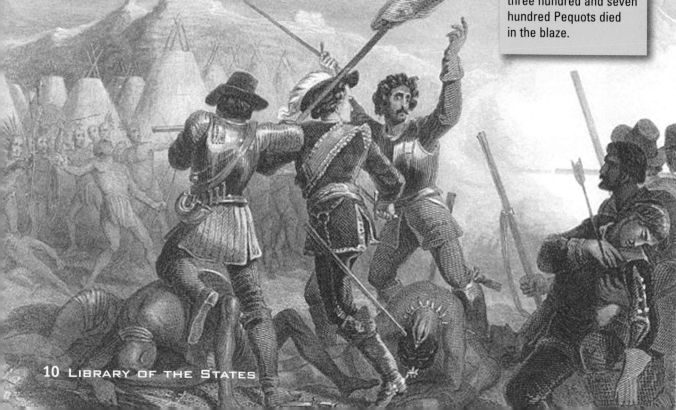

Early Government

Connecticut lawmakers began to focus on setting up a government for their colony in 1638. They adopted the thoughts expressed in Reverend Hooker's sermons and drew up a charter called the Fundamental Orders.

Two decades later, in 1660, Connecticut Governor John Winthrop, Jr., and other colonists feared the colony would be taken over by the Massachusetts Bay Colony or by the Dutch who then controlled New Netherland (later New York). To protect themselves, the settlers drew up a charter, a document that said they had a right to live in Connecticut and to govern themselves.

On May 1, 1662, the General Court of Connecticut received the approved charter from King Charles II of England. John Winthrop was instrumental in getting the charter granted. The charter — the first to be granted to an American colony by an English king — decreed that Connecticut was an independent colony that could elect its own governor and enact its own laws.

After Charles II died in 1685, his brother James, Duke of York, became England's king. James II wanted to take back the charter and create one big colony — the Dominion of New England — in northeastern North America. The king appointed Sir Edmund Andros governor-in-chief of the new dominion. In 1687 Governor Andros stormed into the Hartford meeting house where the Connecticut government met and demanded that the legislators give him the charter so that he could rip it up.

The Connecticut officials spread the charter out on the table, but someone snuffed out the candles in the room. In the confusion and darkness, one lawmaker, probably Captain Joseph Wadsworth, slipped out of the room with the charter and hid it in the hollow of a great oak tree in Hartford. The oak, known later as the Charter Oak, kept the charter safely hidden, and Connecticut held on to its status as an independent colony.

Last of the Mohicans?

Uncas (c. 1588–c. 1683) was a sachem, or leader, of the Mohegan nation, allies of the Pequots. Their alliance fractured when Uncas had a dispute with Sassacus, the Pequot sachem, about Pequot aggression against other native groups. The Mohegans and Pequots also disagreed because Sassacus wanted to ally with the Dutch, while Uncas preferred an alliance with the British. In 1633 Uncas led about two thousand Mohegans away from the Pequot across the Thames River, where they settled in the area that is now Norwich. Throughout his long life Uncas was never able to see his people peacefully settled, as attacks from neighboring nations and the encroachment of non-Native settlers on Mohegan territory continued to plague them. Writer James Fenimore Cooper used Uncas's name for one of the heroes of his novel *The Last of the Mohicans*, although the Mohicans (better known as Mahicans) were an entirely separate group who lived in New York and Massachusetts. Both Mohegan and Mahican mean "wolf." The Mohegan nation was recognized by the federal government in 1994. There are approximately one thousand Mohegans living in the United States today, about six hundred of whom live in Connecticut.

The Revolutionary War

During the American Revolution, Connecticut is thought to have contributed more soldiers to the Continental Army than any other New England state except Massachusetts. Among the Connecticut volunteers was young Nathan Hale, who volunteered to spy against the British and was captured and hanged on September 22, 1776. He is most famous for his last words, "I regret that I have but one life to lose for my country."

As the war ebbed and flowed with the seasons, Connecticut farmers continued to cultivate their lands. Governor Jonathan Trumbull of Connecticut was the only governor to stay in office during the war, and he often sent large quantities of food, clothing, and supplies to George Washington and his troops. The iron works in Salisbury also made small arms and cannons. As a result, Washington called Connecticut "The Provisions State" and Governor Trumbull "Brother Jonathan." Brother Jonathan became another name for colonial patriots during the Revolution.

In 1776, the delegates from Connecticut voted for independence from Great Britain at the Continental Congress in Philadelphia. Roger Sherman of Connecticut, together with John Adams, Thomas Jefferson, Benjamin Franklin, and Robert Livingston, contributed to the writing of the Declaration of Independence. Sherman and three

The Traitor

Born in Norwich, Benedict Arnold led American troops to victory in the 1777 Battle of Saratoga and emerged a Revolutionary War hero. He felt slighted, however, when the Continental Congress did not promote him. He lived above his means and was soon in need of money. By May of 1779, Arnold had accepted a British bribe of £10,000 and a commission in their army in return for military secrets. He defected to the British when his betrayal was discovered by George Washington.

▼ The signing of the Declaration of Independence. Roger Sherman is second from the left in the center.

other Connecticut men — Samuel Huntington, William Williams, and Oliver Wolcott — signed the document.

From Agriculture to Manufacturing

During the late eighteenth century, the population of Connecticut exploded. In 1750, before the Revolutionary War, about 110,000 people lived in Connecticut. In 1790 the first national census revealed that the population of Connecticut had more than doubled since 1750.

Many state residents turned from farming to manufacturing. They opened small factories and mills along the rivers, which provided water power that they used to run their machines. The rivers could also be used to import raw materials and take away the finished products for sale. Connecticut companies began to produce textiles, small firearms, hats, buttons, and clocks.

Whaling was an important part of the state economy in the late eighteenth and early nineteenth century. Whaling ships set out from Connecticut's ports and brought home the stripped carcasses of huge sperm whales. At the time, whale oil was used to light lamps, and whale bones were used to make umbrellas and corsets.

Slavery, the *Amistad*, and the Civil War

Slavery was originally part of the fabric of Connecticut life. Initially, in the 1600s, Europeans, Africans, and Native Americans might all be held as indentured servants. Indentured servants were people who typically worked a period of seven years without pay before being released. Others might be made to serve their entire lives, sometimes as punishment for crimes. Eventually, however, slavery became a hereditary position for Africans in the British colonies. They would be slaves for life; their children, too, would be born into slavery.

All Connecticut citizens, however, did not accept slavery, although not necessarily for humanitarian reasons. When, for example, Connecticut banned the import of slaves in

▲ This 1650 grist mill, originally used to grind corn, was in continuous use for more than 250 years.

Inventive Connecticut

Eli Whitney invented the cotton gin in 1793 and also made assembly-line production possible. In 1836, Samuel Colt created a revolver that was used by U.S. soldiers in the Mexican-American War and became one of the most popular firearms in history. In 1843, Charles Goodyear discovered a way to toughen rubber so that it could be used to make things such as bicycle tires. Samuel Morse, a Yale graduate, invented the telegraph and the Morse code in which messages were transmitted. The first message was sent in 1844. Other Connecticut inventions include the first portable typewriter (1843) and the pay phone (1877).

1774, white laborers were the proponents of the ban. They felt slaves were taking their jobs. In 1784 and later in 1797, legislators in Connecticut wrote laws to ban slavery based on moral grounds. The 1784 Gradual Emancipation Act ordered that slaves become free at age twenty-five. The 1797 act lowered the age to twenty-one.

Events in the nineteenth century further shaped Connecticut's views on slavery and helped strengthen its support for the Union side during the Civil War. In 1839 a ship in Long Island Sound was taken into custody by the U.S. Navy. It was a Spanish slave ship, the *Amistad*, and the Africans aboard had mutinied. They had taken over the ship and attempted to return home, but instead they found themselves on Connecticut's shores.

The Spanish and Cuban governments demanded that the slaves be returned to them. Connecticut residents were not so ready to comply. Roger Sherman Baldwin became the slaves' lawyer and fought for their freedom in court, assisted by former president John Quincy Adams of Massachusetts. The case went before the U.S. Supreme Court, which ruled that the Africans were free. The victory in the *Amistad* case was generally celebrated by Connecticut's citizens.

Connecticut also produced the most famous antislavery book of all time — *Uncle Tom's Cabin* (1852), by Hartford resident Harriet Beecher Stowe.

State Heroine

As a young woman, Prudence Crandall took a brave stand against racism. In 1831, she opened a school for girls in Canterbury and announced that she would be teaching both African-American and white students. Her community was not supportive. When she enrolled her first African-American student in 1833, her neighbors threw stones at the school. Crandall responded by allowing only African-American students to attend her school. She was arrested, put on trial, and acquitted. Local people continued to harass her, and then they destroyed the school building. In 1995, Crandall's courage was recognized when she was designated the official state heroine. Her house is pictured above.

Three days after the Civil War began in April 1861, Connecticut men arrived in Washington, D.C., to sign up to fight for the North and end slavery. More than fifty thousand Nutmeggers joined the Union Army. As in the Revolutionary War, no major battles were fought in Connecticut. Factories in the state, however, made guns, gunpowder, soldiers' uniforms, and shoes. By the end of the war, one-third of the Connecticut soldiers in the Union Army were dead.

The Twentieth Century

During the twentieth century Connecticut factories again armed the country. Factories turned out guns and ammunition for World War I and later contributed airplane engines and parts, airplanes, and submarines for World War II. Defense industries in Connecticut did extremely well during the Korean and Vietnam wars as well. During the second half of the twentieth century, the southwestern part of the state became more suburban, as people who worked in New York City began moving to Connecticut and commuting to work. Some of the suburbs, such as Greenwich and New Canaan, are now among the wealthiest communities in the United States.

As Connecticut became a very costly place to live, some industries left, taking their manufacturing plants to other parts of the country where housing and taxes were cheaper. As manufacturing plants closed, unemployment in the state grew. Cities that were abandoned by departing industries decayed. Some of Connecticut's former great cities — such as Bridgeport and New Haven — saw crime rise along with unemployment. Despite the problems of urban poverty, however, the city of Hartford has prospered as a leader in insurance and financial services.

Although Connecticut's population is not growing as rapidly as the rest of the country, it remains a state filled with well-educated people who have the creativity and ingenuity to become good leaders. In 1981 Hartford elected Thirman Milner mayor, making him the first African-American mayor of a New England city. Milner was the child of a disabled war veteran and a domestic worker and identified strongly with the working poor in his constituency. In 2000, Connecticut senator Joseph Lieberman was chosen to be Vice President Al Gore's running mate in the 2000 presidential election.

Nutmeggers

> "[The state was home to] . . . the clock peddler, the schoolmaster, and the senator. The first gives you the time, the second tells you what to do with it, and the third makes your law and civilization."
>
> — *from* Democracy in America *(1840)*,
> *Alexis de Tocqueville, Historian*

Connecticut ranks twenty-ninth in population and is one of the slowest-growing states in the nation. Only Pennsylvania, West Virginia, North Dakota, and the District of Columbia have fewer immigrants. According to the U.S. Census, there were 3,405,565 people living in Connecticut in 2000, compared with an estimated 3,287,116 in 1990. This increase of about 3.5 percent may be due to the fact that Connecticut is one of the most expensive states in which to live and conduct business; however, Connecticut's average per capita personal income of $40,640 is also one of the highest in the nation.

About three-quarters of Connecticut's land is only sparsely populated. Most Connecticut workers are employed in service industries, and they tend to live predominantly in and around metropolitan areas. Bridgeport is the

Age Distribution in Connecticut
(2000 Census)

0–4	223,344
5–19	702,358
20–24	187,571
25–44	1,032,689
45–64	789,420
65 & over	470,183

Across One Hundred Years
Connecticut's three largest foreign-born groups for 1890 and 1990

1890 ■   1990 ■

Ireland 77,880	Germany 28,176	Canada & Newfoundland 21,231	Italy 33,708	Canada 22,291	Poland 20,469

Total state population: 746,258
Total foreign-born: 183,601 (25%)

Total state population: 3,287,116
Total foreign-born: 279,383 (8%)

Patterns of Immigration

The total number of people who immigrated to Connecticut in 1998 was 7,780. Of that number, the largest immigrant groups were from Jamaica (11%), India (6.1%), and Poland (5.6%).

largest city in Connecticut, with 139,529 people.

Before the first European settlers came to Connecticut in 1633, about 7,000 Native Americans lived in the region. According to the 2000 Census there are 9,639 Native people in the state, or about 0.3 percent of the total Connecticut population.

The first great wave of immigration to Connecticut took place in the 1830s and 1840s, when hundreds of thousands of Irish arrived to work in Connecticut's new factories. They started living around factories in Hartford, Waterbury, and the Naugatuck Valley. Many immigrants from Germany arrived in the 1840s. English, Scottish, and French-Canadian immigrants started moving to Connecticut after the Civil War. Then, in the 1880s, Eastern European and Russian Jews left their homelands after a series of pogroms, or massacres. Italian immigrants arrived in search of work, too. By the early twentieth century, 70 percent of state residents were born overseas or had parents who were immigrants.

Many African Americans left the South after the Civil War and settled in northern states. In the early 1900s, many were working on tobacco farms in Connecticut.

▲ Women in a Bridgeport factory sew flying suits for the U.S. Air Force during World War II. The people of Connecticut have a long-standing tradition of performing defense industry work.

Heritage and Background, Connecticut — Year 2000

▶ Here's a look at the racial backgrounds of Nutmeggers today. Connecticut ranks twenty-second among all U.S. states with regard to African Americans as a percentage of the population.

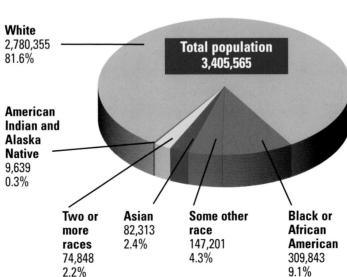

White
2,780,355
81.6%

Total population
3,405,565

American Indian and Alaska Native
9,639
0.3%

Native Hawaiian and other Pacific Islander
1,366
0.04%

Two or more races
74,848
2.2%

Asian
82,313
2.4%

Some other race
147,201
4.3%

Black or African American
309,843
9.1%

Note: 9.4% (320,323) of the population identify themselves as **Hispanic** or **Latino,** a cultural designation that crosses racial lines. Hispanics and Latinos are counted in this category as well as the racial category of their choice.

After World War II, African Americans moved into the state in greater numbers and settled in Connecticut's cities. After 1960, the Latino population began to grow and is still increasing.

Education

The Connecticut Constitution states that "there shall always be free public elementary and secondary schools in the state" and that "the state shall maintain a system of higher education."

Connecticut's Code of 1650 said that settlements of fifty or more families had to provide a schoolmaster for the children. When a town's population grew to one hundred families or more, it had to set up a "grammar school" and prepare the boys for Harvard College, which opened in 1636 in Cambridge, Massachusetts. Harvard was the only major institution of higher education in the area.

Separation of Church and State

The Congregational Church was part of the colonial government until 1818, and Nutmeggers were required to pay taxes to the church, even if they joined a different one. The constitution of 1818 stripped the Congregational Church of its taxing power and declared that all people should be free to attend whichever church they preferred.

Educational Levels of Connecticut Workers (age 25 and over)	
Less than 9th grade	185,213
9th to 12th grade, no diploma	271,995
High school graduate, including equivalency	648,366
Some college, no degree or associate degree	495,696
Bachelor's degree	356,289
Graduate or professional degree	241,404

▼ The skyline of Hartford, Connecticut's capital.

Connecticut settlers soon wanted to create their own college within the colony. In 1701, ten ministers donated books to start one. The Connecticut General Assembly passed a bill to found a local college. The Collegiate School opened the following year. Just one student enrolled, and his classes were conducted in the rector's home. In 1716, the college moved from Killington to New Haven, and in 1718 it was renamed Yale College after Elihu Yale, a merchant who made a large donation to help build the school.

In 1838, the Connecticut General Assembly created a board of commissioners to make sure that all school-age children attended school and that teachers were qualified. By 1868 all elementary schools in Connecticut were free of charge and four years later, most of the public high schools were free, too. As of 1999, more than eight out of ten, or 83.7 percent, of Connecticut residents had their high school diplomas, and one-third of the state's residents had a four-year college degree or more.

Connecticut has two state university systems — the University of Connecticut, with five campuses, and Connecticut State University, with four. The state also has twelve regional community colleges, five technical colleges, and twenty-five private colleges and universities. Yale University, Trinity College in Hartford, and Wesleyan University in Middletown are among these.

Religion

Today, 85 percent of Connecticut residents belong to Christian churches, and half of those belong to Roman Catholic churches. Connecticut Christians also belong to Episcopal, Methodist, Baptist, and Congregational churches, among others. Connecticut has the sixth-largest Jewish population of the fifty states, although Jews account for just 2.4 percent of the total Connecticut population. Among Nutmeggers practicing other faiths, 0.3 percent are Unitarian, 0.2 percent are Buddhist, 0.1 percent are Hindu, and 0.1 percent are Muslim.

▲ Students at Yale University in New Haven celebrate graduation.

School for Native Americans

In 1754, Connecticut minister Reverend Eleazar Wheelock started teaching Native Americans at a school he opened in the town of Columbia, near Lebanon. He called it Moor's Indian Charity School. In 1769, Dr. Wheelock moved his school to New Hampshire, where it was renamed Dartmouth College. It became New Hampshire's first university and one of the seven Ivy League schools.

A Golden Coast

> New England is a high, hilly and in some parts mountainous country formed by nature to be inhabited by a hardy race of free, independent republicans.
>
> — *Jedediah Morse, early U.S. geographer, 1804*

Connecticut is New England's southernmost state. It borders Massachusetts, New York, and Rhode Island. Waves from Long Island Sound and the Atlantic Ocean lap the approximately 278 miles (447 km) of its southern coastline.

The Taconic Mountains in the northwestern corner of the state are part of the Appalachian Mountains. They include the Berkshire Hills and continue on through Massachusetts, New York, and Vermont. Connecticut's highest point, the southern slope of Mount Frissell, lies in the northwestern part of the state. The mountain's summit, however, is in neighboring Massachusetts. A narrow strip of land along Long Island Sound is part of the Coastal Lowlands, a territory extending from Connecticut to Maine. The coastal plain and the Connecticut Valley Lowland are flat. Most of Connecticut's large cities can be found there. Two-thirds of Connecticut, however, is undeveloped land. Northeastern Connecticut is particularly wooded. Pilots say that this hilly stretch of Connecticut is dark as they fly between Boston and Washington, D.C., at night. It is one of the few spots on the East Coast that is not illuminated.

Highest Point
**Mt. Frissell
(southern slope)**
2,380 feet (725 m) above sea level

Largest Lakes
Candlewood Lake
5,420 acres (2,193 ha)

Barkhamsted Reservoir
2,323 acres (941 ha)

Lake Lillinonah
1,300 acres (526 ha)

▼ *From left to right:* farmland in Cheshire; wild turkeys; sailboats off the coast near Noank; autumn foliage; a Connecticut stream; white-tailed deer.

Connecticut's southern beaches are gorgeous. Boating, fishing, and sunbathing are popular on Long Island Sound. Many Nutmeggers, as well as people from other states, spend their summer vacations in cottages or summer homes on the beach. Through the years, proximity to the Atlantic Ocean has enabled many Connecticut residents along the coast to make a living in tourism, shipbuilding, and fishing.

Rivers and Lakes

The Connecticut River is the longest river in all of New England. It starts in New Hampshire and runs through Connecticut before spilling into Long Island Sound at Old Saybrook. Boats can sail from Long Island Sound north to Hartford, beyond which the river is no longer navigable.

The Connecticut River Valley has the richest soil in the state, which is why Native Americans lived there and why the colonists built their first three towns — Windsor, Wethersfield, and Hartford — there. Much of the rest of Connecticut is too rocky and hilly to farm. In the valley, however, farmers have been able to grow vegetables and tobacco, which is used mainly to make cigar wrappers.

The Housatonic is Connecticut's second-longest river. It drains the Berkshires, flowing south through the western part of the state. The Shepaug and Naugatuck Rivers feed into the Housatonic before it empties into Long Island Sound at Stratford. The mouth of the Housatonic is an estuary, or a body of water where the freshwater silt from the uplands mixes with the saltwater of the sea. The estuary supports a great deal of plant and animal life.

There are more than two thousand lakes and ponds in Connecticut. The largest, Candlewood Lake near Danbury, is actually artificial rather than natural. It is popular for boating, swimming, and other recreational sports.

Average January temperature
Bridgeport: 29°F (-2°C)
Hartford: 25° F (-4° C)

Average July temperature
Bridgeport: 74°F (23°C)
Hartford: 73°F (22°C)

Average yearly rainfall
Bridgeport: 42 inches (107 cm)
Hartford: 44 inches (112 cm)

Average yearly snowfall
Bridgeport: 25 inches (64 cm)
Hartford: 51 inches (130 cm)

Major Rivers

Connecticut River
410 miles (660 km)

Housatonic River
149 miles (240 km)

Naugatuck River
40 miles (64 km)

Thames River
15 miles (24 km)

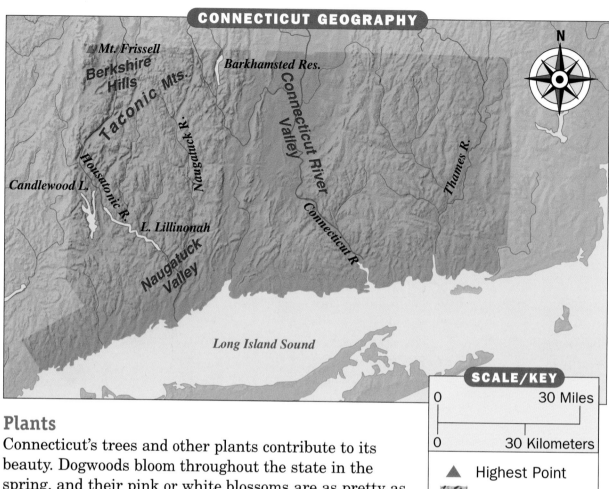

CONNECTICUT GEOGRAPHY

Mt. Frissell

Berkshire Hills

Taconic Mts.

Barkhamsted Res.

Naugatuck R.

Connecticut River Valley

Thames R.

Housatonic R.

Candlewood L.

L. Lillinonah

Connecticut R.

Naugatuck Valley

Long Island Sound

SCALE/KEY

0   30 Miles

0   30 Kilometers

▲ Highest Point

Mountains

Plants

Connecticut's trees and other plants contribute to its beauty. Dogwoods bloom throughout the state in the spring, and their pink or white blossoms are as pretty as the mountain laurel that grows in the woods and along the roads.

Autumn is a special treat. The leaves on Connecticut's ash, beech, birch, elm, hemlock, maple, and oak trees change color, turning dazzling reds, oranges, yellows, and golds.

Animals

By the end of the nineteenth century, bears, moose, deer, beavers, and turkeys could no longer be found in southern New England. Settlers had hunted them or cleared the land of their habitats. Today, however, few residents make their living farming, and land is returning to forest. Now that the state is more than 60 percent forested, animal population numbers are soaring. Deer are the most common, and there are about 76,000 of them in the state, according to the Connecticut Department of Environmental Protection. As late as 1998, Connecticut did not have a native moose population. In recent years, however, moose have been more frequently spotted in Connecticut. There may be as many as fifteen moose that now make Connecticut their home.

In 1975, the state reintroduced wild turkeys in the hope that they would breed. Now as many as thirty thousand are waddling around. Coyotes are making an appearance, too. There are approximately 4,000 to 6,000 coyotes roaming Connecticut. Foxes and bobcats are rare, but they are sometimes seen in the state. At least 100 black bears also make Connecticut home.

Climate

Long Island — part of New York State — and Rhode Island help protect Connecticut from major Atlantic storms. Although there have been severe winter storms, such as the infamous ice storm of 1973, Connecticut's weather is relatively mild. The average January temperature is 26° Fahrenheit (-3° Celsius), and the average July temperature is 71°F (21°C). Temperatures, however, can vary within the state. The temperatures in the northwestern and northeastern hills are sometimes 10 degrees lower than in the Connecticut River Valley. During a winter storm, it is not uncommon for snow to fall in the hilly regions and rain to fall along the coast.

Turning Leaves

The substance that gives leaves their green color and allows them to absorb energy from the Sun is called chlorophyll. As the weather turns cold, deciduous trees (trees that shed their foliage seasonally) cut off water to their leaves to conserve energy. The chlorophyll is no longer necessary, and it starts to break down. Other colors — pigments that have been hidden by the green chlorophyll — are revealed.

The result is a natural spectacle that brings thousands of "leaf-peeping" tourists to Connecticut. The abundance of maple trees in the state means that golds, as well as brilliant reds and oranges, are often visible.

▼ **Northern Connecticut along the Housatonic River Valley.**

Yankee Ingenuity

> A good deal of man's modern movement had begun in Connecticut. The bicycle had begun in America in Hartford. Automobiles had been made there. Both rolled in possibility upon Charles Goodyear's invention of the process of vulcanizing rubber not far from Hartford in Naugatuck, just a hundred years before I rolled in on his invention into Hartford and across the Connecticut River to the United Aircraft plants.
>
> — *Jonathan Daniels, a Southern writer, 1940*

Where does the phrase "Yankee ingenuity" come from? Connecticut. Connecticut inventors created the cotton gin, the portable typewriter, and the sewing machine — all of which made it faster, cheaper, and easier to produce and sell manufactured goods. Eli Whitney not only invented the first cotton gin in 1793 to clean the seed from fiber, but he also came up with the clever idea of producing standard, interchangeable parts so that guns could be made more quickly and at lower cost. In 1843, the first portable typewriter was made in Connecticut. Elias Howe invented the sewing machine in 1846, making the mass production of clothing possible. Yankee ingenuity contributed substantially to industrial growth.

During every war from the Revolutionary War onward, Connecticut armed the nation. Its factories helped make the guns, ammunition, airplane engines and parts, nuclear submarines, and helicopters that U.S. forces relied on in those wars. Even today, manufacturing is one of Connecticut's largest industries, employing more than 20 percent of the state's total workers. Connecticut firms still contribute to the U.S. national defense.

Connecticut also makes some of the United States's favorite things. Take Pez candies, for instance. The plastic novelty holders that dispense the little candies are made in

Top Employers (of workers age sixteen and over)	
Services	32.7%
Manufacturing	20.5%
Wholesale and retail trade	19.6%
Finance, insurance, and real estate	10.4%
Transportation, communications, and public utilities	5.9%
Construction	5.9%
Government	3.7%
Agriculture, forestry, and fisheries	1.2%
Mining	0.1%

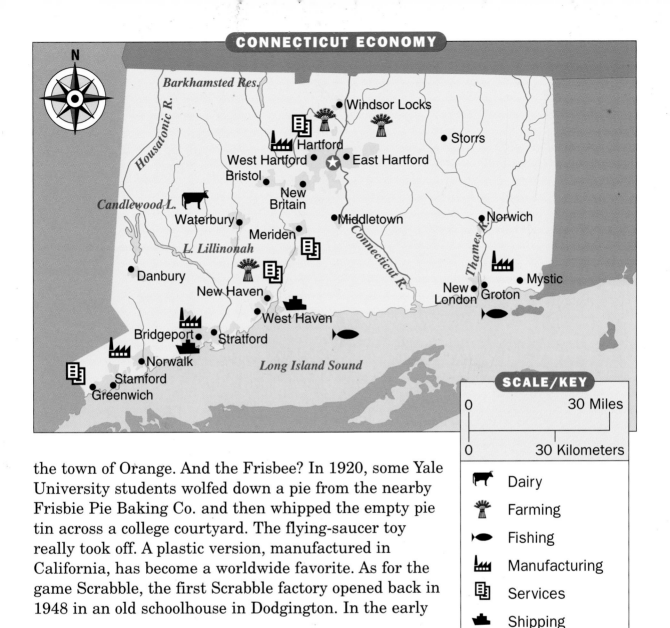

CONNECTICUT ECONOMY

Barkhamsted Res.

Housatonic R.

Windsor Locks

Hartford

Storrs

West Hartford • East Hartford

Bristol

New Britain

Candlewood L.

Waterbury

Meriden

Middletown

Norwich

Thames R.

Connecticut R.

L. Lillinonah

Danbury

New Haven

West Haven

New London • Groton

Mystic

Bridgeport • Stratford

Long Island Sound

Norwalk

Stamford

Greenwich

SCALE/KEY

0   30 Miles

0   30 Kilometers

- Dairy
- Farming
- Fishing
- Manufacturing
- Services
- Shipping
- Urban Areas

the town of Orange. And the Frisbee? In 1920, some Yale University students wolfed down a pie from the nearby Frisbie Pie Baking Co. and then whipped the empty pie tin across a college courtyard. The flying-saucer toy really took off. A plastic version, manufactured in California, has become a worldwide favorite. As for the game Scrabble, the first Scrabble factory opened back in 1948 in an old schoolhouse in Dodgington. In the early

Connecticut Gross State Product   Millions of dollars

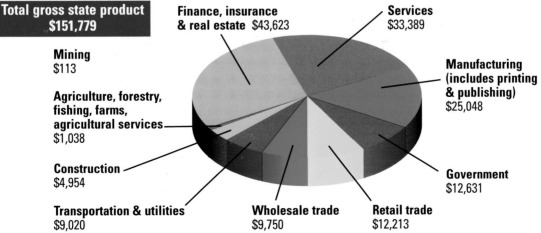

Total gross state product $151,779

Finance, insurance & real estate $43,623

Services $33,389

Mining $113

Manufacturing (includes printing & publishing) $25,048

Agriculture, forestry, fishing, farms, agricultural services $1,038

Construction $4,954

Government $12,631

Transportation & utilities $9,020

Wholesale trade $9,750

Retail trade $12,213

CONNECTICUT **25**

1950s, the president of Macy's department store spotted the game while he was on vacation. With Macy's backing the game quickly became a hit.

Connecticut companies made the first pay phone back in 1877, the lollipop back in 1908, and Silly Putty shortly after World War II.

Transportation

In order for companies to transport all the goods they produce to stores across the nation, they need good roads, railroads, and seaports. Connecticut has all three. Today more than 20,000 miles (32,180 km) of roads and highways run through the state. The main commercial highway is Interstate 95, which runs along the United States's eastern seaboard and connects New York City and Boston, Massachusetts. The Hartford and New Haven Railroad, Connecticut's first important railroad, opened for service between New Haven and Meriden in 1838. Today, four main railroads operate in Connecticut to provide freight service for manufactured goods. At seaports such as Bridgeport and New Haven on Long Island Sound, businesses can load their products to ship them overseas. Bradley International Airport in Windsor Locks ships goods by air. Located near Hartford, it is the state's major airport.

▲ Lollipops, one of Connecticut's inventions.

Agriculture

Although Connecticut has four thousand farms, slightly more than 1 percent of Connecticut workers are engaged in farming. Connecticut's biggest agricultural products are actually shrubs, flowers, and plants that are sold at plant nurseries. Eggs and milk are the most important farm products. Dairy cattle and other livestock are next, followed by shellfish.

Finance and Insurance

Hartford is the insurance capital of the nation. The city is home to fifty insurance companies, including three of the largest insurance firms in the country. Nutmeggers started selling insurance after the Revolutionary War to insure ship owners in case their boats sank or lost their cargo. In 1795, salesmen began selling fire insurance. Later companies added coverage in case of illness or accidents. Today, some companies offer investment and real estate services.

Made in Connecticut

Leading farm products and crops
Nursery/greenhouse plants
Dairy
Mushrooms
Shellfish
Tobacco
Vegetables

Other products
Aircraft engines
Submarines
Helicopters

Major Airports		
Airport	Location	Passengers per year (2000)
Bradley International Airport	Hartford	7,338,744
Tweed New Haven Airport	New Haven	60,000

Manufacturing

Connecticut workers are among the most educated in the nation. This is because the state has the highest percentage of people with college degrees. Education enables Nutmeggers to make their mark in high-tech industries such as computers and defense. The state is a leading manufacturer of aircraft parts, submarines, and helicopters. Connecticut is also the home of United Technologies Corp., formerly the Sikorsky Aero Engineering Corporation, which has been building helicopters in Connecticut since 1929. Pharmaceuticals are another major Connecticut industry, and major pharmaceutical corporations such as Bayer have offices in the state.

Natural Resources

Some clever Connecticut farmers discovered that they could make money by selling the state's poor soil. The stony soil could at least yield stone, and crushed stone has become the state's chief mining product. Sand and gravel, which are used to make roads and concrete, are the next biggest sellers. Connecticut is also rich in garnets, hard minerals used for jewelry and on industrial grinding machines and saws to aid in manufacturing.

Tourism

With Connecticut's charming coastline and pretty New England towns, tourism has become a $4 billion-a-year service industry. The majority of Connecticut workers are employed in the service industry, which includes jobs in hotels, restaurants, or health care facilities. Casinos, such as those run by the Mohegan tribe, are also a major source of revenue.

▼ Groton is known as the "submarine capital of the world" because it is the location of a shipyard where submarines, such as the one below, are built and launched. The U.S. Naval Submarine School is also in Groton.

Power of the People

> As God has given us liberty, let us take it.
> — *Reverend Thomas Hooker, 1638*

A state constitution is a set of laws and principles by which the state government operates. Connecticut has had four constitutions: the Fundamental Orders of 1639, the Charter of 1662, the constitution of 1818, and the present constitution, which was ratified in 1965.

The Fundamental Orders were eleven orders, or laws, that followed the beliefs about government that Reverend Thomas Hooker expressed in a church sermon he gave in 1638. Reverend Hooker felt that qualified people should have the right to choose their public magistrates, or lawmakers, by voting and that the power of these magistrates must be limited. The Fundamental Orders also showed that the Connecticut colonists held no allegiance to England and preferred to set up their own independent government. While Massachusetts had the first state constitution, dating to May 16, 1775, historian John Fisk believes that the Fundamental Orders are "the first written constitution known to history that created a government and it marked the beginning of U.S. democracy."

In 1662, when the king of England claimed that all of the colonies in New England belonged to England, Connecticut settlers quickly drew up the Charter of 1662, which the king signed, thus guaranteeing the colony its right to self-government and its citizens their private property.

The constitution of 1818 removed the Congregational Church's role in state government and decreed that all religions should be given equal status. This constitution also divided the state government into three branches — the executive, legislative, and judicial — each with its own powers. The senate was established as the upper house of the General Assembly, the state's legislature, and the house of representatives was established as the lower house.

Connecticut's population shifted from small towns to

Connecticut Constitution

"**A**ll political power is inherent in the people, and all free governments are founded on their authority, and instituted for their benefit; and they have at all times an undeniable and indefeasible right to alter their form of government in such manner as they may think expedient."

— *From the constitution of the state of Connecticut*

DID YOU KNOW?

The Charter Oak, which sheltered the Connecticut Charter for fourteen years, fell during a storm on August 21, 1856. By that time, the tree was more than two hundred years old.

Elected Posts in the Executive Branch		
Office	Length of Term	Term Limits
Governor	4 years	None
Lieutenant Governor	4 years	None
Secretary of State	4 years	None
Treasurer	4 years	None
Comptroller	4 years	None
Attorney General	4 years	None

larger cities throughout the nineteenth and twentieth centuries, and soon the number of seats in the house and senate no longer reflected the number of people or electors living in each city or town.

The constitution of 1965 fixed this problem by basing representation in the state legislature on population. The state government is now required to use information from the federal census, which is published every ten years, to draw new boundaries for senate voting districts and reapportion the house by revising the number of house representatives each district should get.

The Executive Branch

The governor heads the executive branch. The governor and lieutenant governor are elected as a team to four-year terms. There is no limit to the number of terms they can serve. The governor has the power to appoint the heads of practically all administrative departments, boards, and commissions (except for the commissioners of education and higher education), is in charge of the state budget, and is also commander-in-chief of the National Guard. The guard can be called out by the governor in an emergency. The governor has five days to review a bill and can either sign it, making it a law, or veto it. A two-thirds majority vote of the General Assembly can override a veto. A bill becomes law if the governor fails to take action on it within five days.

The Legislative Branch

The legislative branch of government in Connecticut is called the General Assembly. It is made up of a 36-member senate and a 151-member house of representatives. Members of both houses are elected by the voters to serve two-year terms. The lieutenant governor presides over the senate. The house of representatives elects its own speaker. The main responsibility of the General Assembly is to make laws or constitutional amendments. Bills become laws if they are approved by a majority of the members of both houses and are signed by the governor. The assembly also balances the power of the other two branches of government by having some executive and judicial powers. For example, it approves the governor's appointments, and it can impeach the governor or state judges.

The Judicial Branch

Connecticut's judicial branch is made up of the judicial department and the Division of Public Defender Services. The chief justice is the head of the judicial department. The Connecticut court system is made up of the supreme court, the appellate court, the superior court, and the probate courts. The supreme court is the state's highest court — the state court of last resort for people unhappy with lower court decisions. The supreme court consists of a chief justice and six associate justices. The appellate court is fairly new. It began hearing cases in 1983 to help the supreme court cut down on its heavy caseload. The appellate court consists of nine judges, and the chief justice of the supreme court selects one of them to be chief presiding judge. The superior court is Connecticut's only trial court, and its purpose is to quickly resolve individual conflicts and criminal cases. The superior court consists of 178 judges. All the justices and judges of the state's three highest courts are nominated by the governor and appointed by the General Assembly to serve eight-year terms. Judges are not limited in the number of terms that they can serve, but they must retire at the age of seventy.

DID YOU KNOW?

On January 20, 2001, George Walker Bush placed his left hand on the same Bible that his father, George Herbert Walker Bush, had used when he was sworn in as president twelve years earlier. It was only the second time in U.S. history that a son followed his father to the White House. John Quincy Adams was the first son to do so, in 1825. Adams, the sixth president, was the son of John Adams, the second president.

General Assembly			
House	**Number of Members**	**Length of Term**	**Term Limits**
Senate	36 senators	2 years	None
House of Representatives	151 representatives	2 years	None

GEORGE HERBERT WALKER BUSH (1989–1993)

Although born in Massachusetts, George H. W. Bush moved with his family to Greenwich, Connecticut, when he was less than one year old. During World War II, Bush, at age eighteen, became the Navy's youngest pilot. In 1944, Japanese soldiers shot down Bush's plane. Bush bombed an island radio station before parachuting into the ocean and received the Distinguished Flying Cross for his heroism. After entering politics in the 1960s as a Texas Republican, Bush served two terms in the U.S. House of Representatives. In July 1980, Ronald Reagan invited Bush to be his vice-presidential running mate. The two were elected for two terms. Bush himself won the presidency in 1988, becoming the ninth U.S. vice president to be elected president. Four years later, in 1992, Governor Bill Clinton of Arkansas defeated Bush in his bid for reelection.

GEORGE WALKER BUSH (2001–)

George W. Bush was born in New Haven, Connecticut, but, like his father, his career in politics began in Texas. Bush was elected the forty-sixth governor of Texas in 1994. Four years later he was reelected, becoming the first governor in Texas history to win two consecutive terms.

In 2000, Bush ran for the presidency. The day after the 2000 presidential election, the United States did not know if Bush or Vice President Al Gore was its forty-third president. The election was so close that it came down to the state of Florida. Whoever won that state's twenty-five electoral votes would be the nation's next president. Thirty-six days later, the U.S. Supreme Court ordered an end to Florida's ballot recounting, and Bush was declared the winner of Florida, although Gore won the nationwide popular vote in one of the closest presidential elections in U.S. history.

◄ Chief Justice William Rehnquist administers the oath of office to George H. W. Bush. At left, George W. Bush, future president, looks on.

The lowest courts in Connecticut are the 130 probate courts, each of which serves only the people living in its district. Probate courts decide cases involving wills, trust funds, parental rights, legal guardians, adoptions, and people who are mentally ill. Probate judges are elected to four-year terms by the voters in their districts.

Connecticut Sights and Sounds

> This was the most delightful ride I ever remembered to have taken, more beautiful scenery in that distance than in any part of my travels; the whole a most romantic country, thickly settled, highly cultivated, and adorned both by nature and art.
>
> —*William Loughton Smith,*
> *on a tour of Connecticut in 1790*

In addition to enjoying an important historical role and rich traditions, Connecticut benefits from bordering two other New England states — Massachusetts and Rhode Island — as well as New York. Those who take ferry rides to nearby islands, visit museums, or tour Revolutionary War sites in the state find both New England charm and New England history. An abundance of Broadway-bound shows offers Nutmeggers a taste of the culture found in New York City, which has a skyline that can be seen from some places along the Connecticut shore.

Leisure in Art

From 1885 to 1930, many U.S. painters set up their easels in Connecticut's quaint villages or along its beaches.

▼ Trolleys, or streetcars, like this one provided transportation to the citizens of Connecticut from the late 1870s to the mid-twentieth century. This particular car was active in New Haven and became the last trolley car of its kind to operate for actual fares, retiring in 1940.

Dabbing at their canvases with bright colors and short strokes, they practiced the style developed in France known as Impressionism. Connecticut practitioners of the style, such as Childe

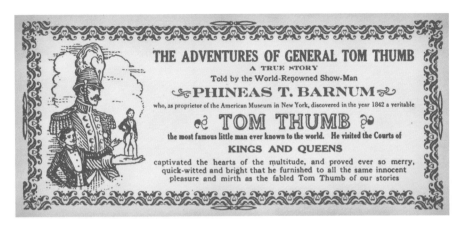

Hassam, were known as Cos Cob Impressionists, after Cos Cob, the town on the shore where they liked to paint. Connecticut museums that display works of Cos Cob Impressionists include the Bruce Museum in Greenwich, the Hill-Stead Museum in Farmington, and the New Britain Museum of American Art. Paintings by such famous French Impressionists as Auguste Renoir, Claude Monet, and Edgar Degas hang in the Yale University Art Gallery. Yale's gallery, which was founded in 1832, is the oldest university art museum in the country. It also exhibits important works by Vincent Van Gogh and Pablo Picasso.

▲ Circus owner and impresario P. T. Barnum drew crowds to his shows with intriguing advertising, such as this handbill for an appearance by Charles Stratton, whose stage name was Tom Thumb.

Theater lovers can keep very busy seeing musicals, dramas, and touring shows throughout the state. Many plays appearing at the Long Wharf Theatre or Yale Repertory Theatre in New Haven go on to Broadway in New York City. Plays at Stamford's Rich Forum and Palace Theater do, too. The Goodspeed Opera House in East Haddam still stages musicals in its nineteenth-century Victorian theater overlooking the Connecticut River. Many of its shows have also moved on to Broadway.

Since 1931, famous actors have starred on the stage at the historic Westport Country Playhouse. The Shubert Performing Arts Center in New Haven offers plays, dance, and opera to interested theatergoers.

Libraries and Museums

The Yale Peabody Museum is one of the largest museums of natural history in New England. The museum holds meteorites, mummies, an Apatosaurus that is 67 feet (20 m) long, and the remains of a seventy-five-million-year-old turtle.

Not far away is the Shore Line Trolley Museum in East Haven, where visitors can hop aboard and ride any one of

DID YOU KNOW?

Theodate Pope Riddle (1867–1946) became one of the United States's first important female architects. She designed a retirement home in Farmington for her parents in 1898 that is now used by the Hill-Stead Museum. Pope, who lived much of her life in Connecticut, also designed the Westover School in Middlebury.

a hundred antique trolleys. In the town of Essex, the Essex Steam Train & Riverboat Ride takes visitors back in time. The open railroad coaches from the 1920s are pulled by a real steam locomotive.

The New England Air Museum in Windsor Locks is the largest aviation museum in the Northeast. Among other aeronautical objects, it exhibits a balloon basket from the 1870s that is the oldest piece of U.S. aircraft still in existence.

The Beardsley Zoo in Bridgeport is the state's only zoo. The 52-acre (21-ha) zoo is home to timber wolves, antelope, ocelots, and bison. Bridgeport is also home to the Barnum Museum. Among other displays, this museum features a model of a circus with a half million figures.

In Madison, Hammonasset Beach State Park has a 2-mile (3-km) stretch of beach — the largest public beach in Connecticut. Up the coast lies Mystic Seaport, which is a re-creation of a nineteenth-century whaling village. Founded in 1929 on an old shipyard, this "museum of the sea" is a research center as well as a center for the preservation of seafaring skills. Visitors may board a collection of boats from the nineteenth and early twentieth centuries. Not far away is the Mystic Aquarium, which houses some 3,500 creatures gathered from the world's oceans. The Maritime Aquarium at Norwalk has an

▲ *(Top)* A bottle-nosed dolphin at the Mystic Aquarium. *(Inset)* A replica of the first hot air balloon rests near the New England Air Museum in Windsor Locks.

IMAX theater, touch tanks, and an educational maze. The aquarium focuses on marine life in and around Long Island Sound.

The 1868 Sheffield Island Lighthouse is located off the coast at Norwalk and can be visited by taking a thirty-minute ferry ride out to sea. Legend has it that Captain Kidd, the famous pirate, hid from the British on the Thimble Islands off the coast of Branford, where he also buried his treasure. Visitors can ride ferries to the islands.

Sports

Connecticut does not have any major-league football, baseball, or basketball teams, and, since the departure of the Hartford Whalers, also has no major-league hockey team. It does, however, boast the University of Connecticut (UConn) Huskies. UConn has won one National Collegiate Athletic Association (NCAA) men's national basketball championship, in 1999, and three women's national basketball championships since 1995, including the title in 2002. That year, the women's team won an amazing thirty-nine games without a single loss and laid claim to being perhaps the greatest women's college team ever. UConn also won the 2000 NCAA national men's soccer championship.

Connecticut hosts the Bridgeport Barrage, one of six teams to play in the first season of major-league lacrosse. This professional outdoor league started in 2001.

As for other pro sports, Connecticut hosts the annual Canon Greater Hartford Open, a tournament on the Professional Golfers' Association (PGA) Tour that draws top golfers every year.

Connecticut also boasts a professional tennis franchise, the Hartford FoxForce. The FoxForce features world-ranked players, such as Monica Seles, who take time out every summer to compete in the DuPont World Team Tennis League. Connecticut tennis fans can also see their favorite professional women tennis players at the annual Pilot Pen International Women's Championships, held every August in New Haven.

▼ The University of Connecticut's powerhouse women's basketball team takes on St. John's in 1995.

Connecticut also fields a number of minor-league teams in several sports, including baseball (in the Eastern League and the Atlantic League), hockey (in the American Hockey League), and football (in the Arena Football League's developmental league).

Connecticut's Olympians

Connecticut has nurtured some Olympic gold medal winners through the years. Lindy Remigino, a graduate of Hartford Public High School, took home two gold medals in track and field from the 1952 Games. Two Connecticut athletes won gold medals in 1976. Dorothy Hamill of Riverside won the medal for figure skating, and Bruce Jenner, who went to high school in Newtown, won the gold medal for the decathlon.

Kristine Lilly of Wilton played for the U.S. women's national soccer team that won the gold medal in 1996, the first year that soccer was an Olympic sport. Lilly also helped the women's team win the Women's World Cup in 1999. Today, Lilly starts for the Boston Breakers in the Women's United Soccer Association (WUSA), the first women's professional soccer league in the nation.

Historic Sites

On September 6, 1781, Benedict Arnold, having betrayed the United States at West Point, compounded his treachery by leading British troops against American soldiers at Fort Griswold, today the Fort Griswold Battlefield State Park in Groton. A museum and a monument to

◄ A Connecticut man demonstrates nineteenth-century blacksmithing techniques at Mystic Seaport.

A Matter of Time

Bristol was the nation's center for clock- and watchmaking in the nineteenth century. The first clock factory in the country was established there in 1790, and the town seal even has a clock face in its center. Famous clockmaker Seth Thomas began making clocks in nearby Plymouth Hollow in 1813, and the town changed its name to Thomaston to honor him in 1875.

Connecticut is filled with historic places and buildings, such as the Nathan Hale Schoolhouse (*inset*) in East Haddam, where this national hero taught in 1773–1774. (*Left*) This room is one of nineteen in Mark Twain's Hartford mansion. One of the most influential writers in America, Twain wrote two of his most famous novels, *The Adventures of Tom Sawyer* and *The Adventures of Huck Finn*, while living there.

the more than eighty-two patriots who died in the bloody battle now stand on the site.

In that same year, 1781, General George Washington and Count de Rochambeau of France met at the home of Joseph Webb in Wethersfield to plan the final stages of the Revolutionary War that would finally force England to surrender. The Webb House is now a museum. During the war, Connecticut jailed British soldiers and Tories, or those who sympathized with the British, in Old Newgate Prison in East Granby. Newgate was the first state prison in the United States and is now a museum.

In New Haven, the Grove Street Cemetery contains the graves of Noah Webster, Eli Whitney, Charles Goodyear, and Harriet Beecher Stowe. The cemetery dates back to 1797.

The Nathan Hale Homestead is in South Coventry, and the Nathan Hale Schoolhouses, where Hale taught school from 1773–1775, are in East Haddam and New London.

DID YOU KNOW?

Tapping Reeve House in Litchfield, which opened in 1782, was America's first law school. The Reverend Whitfield House in Guilford, which was built in 1639, is the oldest stone building in New England.

Famous Nutmeggers

> There is little hope of conquering an enemy whose very schoolboys are capable of valor equaling that of trained veterans . . .
>
> — *A captured British sea captain, referring to Connecticut during the Revolutionary War*

Following are only a few of the thousands of people who were born, died, or spent much of their lives in Connecticut and made extraordinary contributions to the state and the nation.

REVEREND THOMAS HOOKER
MINISTER AND STATESMAN

BORN: *July 7, 1586, Leicestershire, England*
DIED: *July 7, 1647, Hartford*

In 1636, Reverend Thomas Hooker and most of his congregation left the Massachusetts Bay Colony. Hooker wanted more of the community's decisions to be determined by the vote of church members rather than by church leaders. On May 31, 1638, he delivered the sermon that would make him famous and that would one day be echoed by Thomas Jefferson, the author of the Declaration of Independence. Hooker said that "the choice of public magistrates belongs unto the people" and that "the foundation of authority is laid, firstly, in the free consent of the people." In other words, if there was to be a government in the Connecticut Colony, Hooker wanted a "general council, chosen by all." Hooker was a great thinker and an extraordinarily powerful speaker and is considered the "father" of Connecticut.

JONATHAN TRUMBULL
POLITICIAN

BORN: *October 12, 1710, Lebanon*
DIED: *August 17, 1785, Lebanon*

When Jonathan Trumbull was elected governor of the Connecticut Colony in 1769, he began what would be a fourteen-year term. The people adored him. General George Washington did, too. When the Revolutionary War broke out, Trumbull cheered on the patriots and did everything he could to help Washington fight the war. When Washington wrote in a letter that he was desperate for more food for his soldiers, Trumbull rounded up a herd of cattle and made sure the herd reached Washington's troops, even in a blizzard. When Washington said he didn't have enough shoes or coats for his soldiers, Trumbull found some. His wife even ripped up a red coat given to her by a French general. She used the cloth to make uniforms for the patriots. Often when Washington wondered what action to take during the war, he was heard to say, "We must consult Brother Jonathan."

ROGER SHERMAN
STATESMAN

BORN: *April 19, 1721, Newton, MA*
DIED: *July 23, 1793, New Haven*

Roger Sherman was a shoemaker, a surveyor, a storekeeper, a lawyer, the treasurer of Yale College, and a judge before he became one of three delegates from Connecticut to the second Continental Congress, where he helped draft both the Declaration of Independence and the Articles of Confederation. At the 1787 Constitutional Convention — where the Constitution of the United States was written — Sherman came up with a compromise that solved the states' biggest concern: the number of representatives each would have. States with bigger populations wanted to elect more representatives to the Senate and House of Representatives. Smaller states were afraid that their votes would be unimportant if the larger states had more votes. Sherman came up with the clever idea of electing an equal number of senators from each state but basing the number of each state's representatives on that state's population. The Connecticut Compromise satisfied the states,

and the Constitution was approved. Sherman is the only person in history who signed the Declaration of Independence, the Articles of Confederation, and the United States Constitution.

NATHAN HALE
PATRIOT

BORN: *June 6, 1755, Coventry*
DIED: *September 22, 1776, New York, NY*

Captain Nathan Hale was a brave patriot who fought in the Revolutionary War. A graduate of Yale and a schoolteacher, Hale volunteered for dangerous missions — including spying on the British in New York City. There Hale was caught drawing sketches of and taking notes on British positions. Although he was only twenty-one, the British Army hanged Hale as a spy. Just before he died, Hale uttered one of the most famous lines in U.S history: "I regret that I have but one life to lose for my country."

NOAH WEBSTER
LEXICOGRAPHER

BORN: *October 16, 1758, West Hartford*
DIED: *May 28, 1843, New Haven*

When Noah Webster taught elementary school in the 1780s, people in the United States spelled the same words many different ways and often used the old method of spelling from England — such as *colour* instead of *color*. Webster wanted his young country to have its own spelling, grammar, and vocabulary. Webster published *The American Spelling Book* in 1783. He began writing the *American Dictionary of the English Language* in 1807. First published in 1828 in three volumes, Webster's dictionary created a national standard for the spelling, pronunciation, meaning, and usage of words, and it introduced new words for animals, plants, and objects that were native to North America. For instance, names now existed for the country's plants, such as corn and squash, and its animals, such as antelope and skunk. The book included more than 12,000 words that had never before been in a dictionary.

ELI WHITNEY
INVENTOR

BORN: *December 8, 1765, Westboro, MA*
DIED: *January 8, 1825, New Haven*

At twelve Eli Whitney made a violin. As a teenager he was a nail maker, a blacksmith, and a hatpin maker. In 1793, one year after he graduated from Yale, Eli Whitney invented the cotton gin — the machine for which he is famous to this day. His cotton "gin" (short for engine) quickly removed the seed from cotton bolls. Whitney's machine was so fast that it cleaned as much cotton in one day as would normally require the work of fifty people.

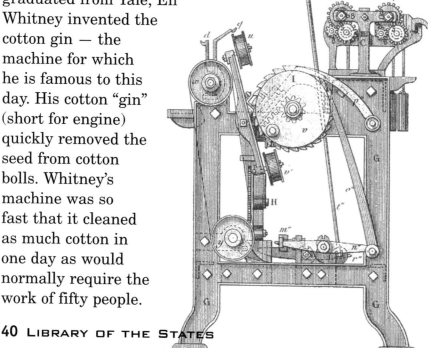

The cotton gin made cotton more profitable to grow, and it turned the United States into the leading cotton-growing nation in the world. Whitney established a gun factory near New Haven in 1798. There he introduced the innovation of interchangeable parts as a way to speed mass production. The factory produced muskets, but the system could be used to produce many other manufactured items as well. Whitney's system of interchangeable parts eventually would evolve into the elaborate assembly lines used in factories to this day.

P. T. BARNUM
CIRCUS IMPRESARIO

BORN: *July 5, 1810, Bethel*
DIED: *April 7, 1891, Bridgeport*

By 1872, Phineas Taylor Barnum was calling his Grand Traveling Museum, Menagerie, Caravan, and Circus "The Greatest Show on Earth." Barnum himself proved to be one of the greatest showmen who ever lived. He called himself the "Prince of Humbug" because he loved to play practical jokes and delight a crowd. In 1841, he bought the American Museum in New York City and amused audiences with curiosities. In 1887, Barnum and James Bailey joined their circuses together to create the Barnum and Bailey Circus.

HARRIET BEECHER STOWE
WRITER

BORN: *June 14, 1811, Litchfield*
DIED: *July 1, 1896, Hartford*

Harriet Beecher Stowe wrote many books, but she became famous for *Uncle Tom's Cabin*, an antislavery novel that was first published in 1852. The book — with its famous characters Uncle Tom, Little Eva, Topsy, and Simon Legree — portrayed the cruelty of slavery. The book angered the proslavery South, and Stowe was hated there. Many in the North, however, welcomed her tale and became more determined than ever to end slavery. Stowe was the daughter of a famous Congregational minister, Lyman Beecher, and sister of Henry Ward Beecher, a famous Presbyterian minister. Her sister Catherine was an early advocate of women's education and domestic science. Stowe wrote other books describing life in New England during the late 1700s and early 1800s. The books also revealed the positive and negative sides of Puritanism.

MARK TWAIN
WRITER

BORN: *November 30, 1835, Florida, MO*
DIED: *April 21, 1910, Redding*

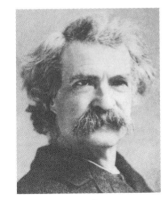

Samuel Langhorne Clemens grew up in Hannibal, Missouri, a small town on the Mississippi River. As a child, he played on the riverbank and was particularly interested in the steamboats that traveled the river.

Clemens's childhood memories would one day provide material for the stories he told in books. In 1847, when he was twelve, Clemens's father died and he went to work for a local newspaper. He worked as a reporter and editor for many years and also learned to pilot steamboats. In 1863, he began to write under the name Mark Twain. Clemens married, and in 1874, he moved with his wife, Olivia, and their children to Hartford. Here, in a beautiful house that he and his wife had built, Twain wrote *The Adventures of Tom Sawyer*, *The Adventures of Huckleberry Finn*, and *A Connecticut Yankee in King Arthur's Court*, all novels that have become international classics.

ELLA GRASSO
POLITICIAN

BORN: *May 10, 1919, Windsor Locks*
DIED: *February 5, 1981, Hartford*

In 1975, Ella Grasso, the daughter of an Italian immigrant baker, became the first woman as well as the first Italian-American governor of Connecticut. She was also the first woman in the United States to be elected governor without having been married to a previous governor. Grasso was a Democrat. She worked for mental health care reform and civil rights. She worked hard at mingling with her constituents and listening to their concerns. Elected to a second four-year term as governor, she retired from office in 1980 with two months to go. She was suffering from cancer and died the following year.

Connecticut

History At-A-Glance

1614
Captain Adriaen Block sails up the Connecticut River, making him the first European to explore the Connecticut region.

1633
The Dutch build a trading fort in Hartford, and English settlers found the town of Windsor.

1636
The towns of Windsor, Wethersfield, and Hartford unite to form the Connecticut Colony.

1637
About ninety colonists attack and burn a large Pequot village in West Mystic, killing more than three hundred.

1639
Leaders of the Connecticut Colony adopt the Fundamental Orders of Connecticut.

1702
The Collegiate School opens. In 1718 it is renamed Yale College.

1764
The *Connecticut Courant* publishes its first newspaper. It later changes its name to the *Hartford Courant*.

1776
Nathan Hale is executed by the British for spying and becomes a Revolutionary War hero.

1784
Connecticut passes the first Gradual Emancipation Act.

1787
The Connecticut Compromise, proposed by Roger Sherman, allows the U.S. Constitution to be approved.

1793
Eli Whitney of New Haven invents the cotton gin, which separates cotton fiber from seed.

1818
The Congregational Church is stripped of its power by a new state constitution.

1600   **1700**   **1800**

1492
Christopher Columbus comes to New World.

1607
Capt. John Smith and three ships land on the Virginia coast and start first English settlement in New World — Jamestown.

1754–63
French and Indian War.

1773
Boston Tea Party.

1776
Declaration of Independence adopted July 4.

1777
Articles of Confederation adopted by Continental Congress.

1787
U.S. Constitution written.

1812–14
War of 1812.

United States

History At-A-Glance

1828
Noah Webster of West Hartford publishes the first dictionary in the United States.

1841
The United States Supreme Court rules that the African slaves who seized control of the ship *Amistad* should be set free and allowed to return home.

1833
Prudence Crandall admits African-American students to her school for girls, angering many Nutmeggers. The school soon closes.

1842
Wadsworth Atheneum, the first free art museum in the nation, opens in Hartford.

1846
Elias Howe invents the sewing machine.

1852
Harriet Beecher Stowe's *Uncle Tom's Cabin* is published.

1856
The Charter Oak, which sheltered the Connecticut Charter for fourteen years before the Revolutionary War, falls in a storm.

1875
Hartford becomes the sole state capital.

1954
The first nuclear submarine in the world launches from the U.S. Naval Base at Groton.

1974
Ella Grasso is elected governor, the first woman governor in the U.S. who has not been preceded in the post by her husband.

1981
Thirman Milner of Hartford becomes the first African-American mayor of a New England city.

2000
Connecticut senator Joseph Lieberman becomes the first Jew to run for U. S. vice president on the ticket of a major party.

1800   **1900**   **2000**

1848
Gold discovered in California draws eighty thousand prospectors in the 1849 Gold Rush.

1861–65
Civil War.

1869
Transcontinental railroad completed.

1917–18
U.S. involvement in World War I.

1929
Stock market crash ushers in Great Depression.

1941–45
U.S. involvement in World War II.

1950–53
U.S. fights in the Korean War.

1964–73
U.S. involvement in Vietnam War.

2000
George W. Bush wins the closest presidential election in history.

2001
A terrorist attack in which four hijacked airliners crash into New York City's World Trade Center, the Pentagon, and farmland in western Pennsylvania leaves thousands dead or injured.

▼ Bridgeport's police department, circa 1914.

Festivals and Fun for All

Check web site for exact date and directions.

American Heritage Festival, Wethersfield

A celebration of the town's history that features the reenactment of a battle from the Revolutionary War, a fife and drum corps, and lantern-light and museum tours.
www.wethersfieldfestival.com

Ancient Evening Graveyards Tour, Farmington

A haunting hike through two graveyards in Farmington, followed by dinner in a former colonial tavern.
www.charteroaktree.com

Apple Harvest Festival, Southington

This street festival on or around Town Green Street celebrates the apple harvest with treats such as fritters and crisps, a carnival, arts and crafts, a road race, and a parade.
www.southingtoncoc.com/AppleFestival.htm

Barnum Festival and Parade, Bridgeport

This annual festival takes place in late spring and celebrates the eclectic glory of P. T. Barnum's life with a parade, a polo match, a classic car show, the Ringmaster's Ball, and contests related to Barnum's career, such as the annual Tom Thumb contest for elementary schoolchildren.
www.barnumfestival.com

Christmas Town Festival, Bethlehem

Hayrides, carolers, and Santa himself make this a holiday treat each year. Best of all, you can visit the Bethlehem post office to mail your Christmas cards with special Christmas cachets and hand-stamped postmarks.
www.ci.bethlehem.ct.us

Durham Fair, Durham

It's an old-time country fair set in a quaint New England village. There are country music performers to entertain and thousands of exhibits.
www.durhamfair.com

Great Connecticut Jazz Festival, Guilford

Top bands from around the world perform favorite Dixieland tunes at the Guilford Fairgrounds.
www.ctjazz.org

International Festival of Arts & Ideas, New Haven

Connecticut's best showcase of performing arts and visual arts, with an exploration of ideas.
www.artidea.org

Litchfield Jazz Festival, Goshen

World-class jazz with arts and crafts and great food and drink.
www.litchfieldjazzfest.com/Programs/JazzFest

Lobsterfest, Mystic

An old-fashioned, outdoor lobster bake on the banks of the Mystic River.
www.mysticseaport.org

Mark Twain Days, **Hartford**

Celebrate Mark Twain and Hartford's Victorian heritage with frog-jumping contests, fireworks, outdoor concerts, and educational activities.
www.marktwaindays.org

Mashantucket Pequot Thames River Fireworks, **Ledyard**

A sound and sight extravaganza on the Thames River. It is one of the largest fireworks displays in the country.
www.sailfest.org/fireworks.html

Mystic Outdoor Art Festival, **Mystic**

More than three hundred artists display their work along the sidewalk in Mystic's historic downtown. There is food and entertainment, too.
www.mysticchamber.org/indmoaf.html

Norwalk Oyster Festival, **Norwalk**

This annual fall event celebrates Long Island Sound's seafaring past. It is packed with local entertainment, arts and crafts, boats, waterfront shows, food, and fireworks.
www.seaport.org/oysterpages/oyster.html

Sound Winds Kite Festival, **Madison**

Hundreds of colorful kites soar and race above the state's longest beach at Hammonassett Beach State Park.
www.middlesexhealth.org/soundwinds

Stamford Parade Spectacular, **Stamford**

This two-hour balloon parade features more than thirty giant, helium-filled character balloons and more than sixty marching bands and floats.
www.stamford-downtown.com/events/cablevision_11_2001

Taste of Hartford, **Hartford**

Local restaurants participate in one of New England's largest outdoor food festivals, complete with live entertainment.
www.tasteofhartford.com

....
▼ The Sound Winds Kite Festival in Madison.

Books

Fritz, Jean. *Harriet Beecher Stowe and the Beecher Preachers*. New York: Putnam Publishing Group, 1998. Connecticut resident Harriet Beecher Stowe was one of the most famous writers of her day. This biography tells the story of her life and of her famous father and siblings.

Larkin, Susan G. *The Cos Cob Art Colony: Impressionists on the Connecticut Shore*. New Haven: Yale University Press, 2001. This volume offers an in-depth look at one of the nation's less well-known artistic movements. A rich sampling of 78 color and 67 black and white reproductions takes the reader on an artistic journey through this turn-of-the-century bohemian community.

Lough, Loree. *Nathan Hale (Revolutionary War Leaders)*. Philadelphia, PA: Chelsea House, 2000. The adventurous and true tale of this great Revolutionary War hero. Primary sources included in the text reinforce the lesson that truth can be more thrilling than fiction.

Murphy, Jim. *The American Revolution as Experienced by One Boy*. Boston, MA: Houghton Mifflin, 1996. About Joseph Plumb Martin from Connecticut, who enlisted in the Continental Army at the age of fifteen. Jim Murphy uses excerpts from Martin's diary to recreate his experience as a young soldier in the midst of the American Revolution.

Web Sites

▶ The official Connecticut state web site
www.state.ct.us

▶ The official state capital web site
www.ci.hartford.ct.us

▶ Connecticut Office of Tourism web site
www.ctbound.org

Note: Page numbers in *italics* refer to maps, illustrations, or photographs.

New Haven, Connecticut, 6, 19, 29
Newgate prison, 37
nickname of Connecticut, 4
Nipmunk Indians, 8
Norwalk Oyster Festival, 45

P
Paucatuck Indians, 8
Paugussett Indians, 8
Peabody Museum, 33
Pequot Indians, 8, 10, 11
Pez candies, 24–25
pharmaceutical industry, 27
plants, 22
Podunk Indians, 8
politics and political figures
　Adams, John Quincy, 14
　Andros, Edmund, 11
　Arnold, Benedict, 12, 36
　Bush, George H. W., 4, 30, *31*
　Bush, George W., 4, 30, *31*
　Charles II, 11
　elected offices, 29
　executive branch, 29
　Fisk, John, 28
　governmental structure, 28–31
　Grasso, Ella, 41
　Hooker, Thomas, 4, 10, 28, 38
　Huntington, Samuel, 12
　James, Duke of York, 11
　judicial branch, 30–31
　legislative branch, 30
　Lieberman, Joseph, *15*
　Milner, Thirman, 15
　Rochambeau, Count de, 37
　separation of church and state, 18
　Sherman, Roger, 39
　Trumbull, Jonathan, 12, 38–39
　Wadsworth, Joseph, 11
　Washington, George, 37, 38–39
　Williams, William, 13
　Winthrop, John, Jr., 11
　Wolcott, Oliver, 13

population, 6
Puritans, 9
Putnam Memorial State Park, 7

Q
Quinnipiac Indians, 8

R
racial makeup of Connecticut, 17–18
railroads, 26
rainfall, 21
recreation, *20*, 21
Rehnquist, William, 31
religion, 4, 9, 18, 19
Remigino, Lindy, 36
Reverend Whitfield House, 37
Revolutionary War (American Revolution), 5, 12–13, 37
revolvers, 13
Rich Forum, 33
Riddle, Theodate Pope, 33
rivers, *20*, 21
roads, 26
Rochambeau, Count de, 37
Roger Sherman (ship), *9*

S
Salisbury, Connecticut, 12
Sassacus Indians, 11
Saukiog Indians, 8
Schaghticoke Indians, 8
Scrabble, 25
seal of Connecticut, *28*
seaports, *8–9*, 26, *32*, 34, 36
Senate, 28, 30
settlers, 8–10
Sheffield Island Lighthouse, *4–5*, 35
shellfish (state), 6
Shepaug River, 21
Sherman, Roger, 39
shipyards, *27*
Shore Line Trolley Museum, 33–34
Shubert Performing Arts Center, 33
Shuckburgh, Richard, 7
slavery, 13–15
Smith, William Loughton, 32

snowfall, 21, 23
Sound Winds Kite Festival, *45*
sports, 35–36
Stamford, Connecticut, 6, *19*
Stamford Parade Spectacular, 45
state university systems, 19
statehood, 6
Stowe, Harriet Beecher, 4, 14, 37, *41*
Stratton, Charles (Tom Thumb), 33
submarines, *27*

T
Taconic Mountains, 20
Tapping Reeve House, 37
Taste of Hartford, 45
telegraph, 13
temperature, 21, 23
tennis, 35–36
Thames River, 21
theater, 33
Thimble Islands, 35
Thomas, Seth, 36
time line of Connecticut history, *42–43*
Tocqueville, Alexis de, 16
tourism, 27
transportation, 26
tree (state), 6
trees, *23*
Trumbull, Jonathan, 12, 38–39
Tunxis Indians, 8
Twain, Mark, 4, *41*
Tweed New Haven Airport, 27

U
Uncas, 8, 11
Uncle Tom's Cabin (Stowe), 14, 41
unemployment, 15
U. S. Constitution, 39
U.S. Naval Submarine School, *27*
United Technologies Corp., 27
University of Connecticut, 19
University of Connecticut Huskies, *35*

V
voting rights, 12

W
Wadsworth, Joseph, 11
Wadsworth Atheneum Museum of Art, 7
wartime industry, 15, *17*, 24
Washington, George, 37, 38–39
water sports, *20*
Waterbury, Connecticut, 6
waterways, *5*
Webb, Joseph, 37
Webb House, 37
Webster, Noah, 7, 37, 39–40
Westport Country Playhouse, 33
Wethersfield, Connecticut, 21
Wethersfield Festival, 45
whaling, 13, 34
Wheelock, Eleazar, 19
Whitney, Eli, 4, 13, 24, 37, 40
wildlife, *20, 21, 22*–23
Williams, William, 13
Windsor, Connecticut, 10, 21
Winthrop, John, Jr., 11
Wolcott, Oliver, 13
Won't Work Theatre, 33

Y
Yale, Elihu, 19
Yale Repertory Theatre, 33
Yale University, 7, 19
"Yankee Doodle," 4, 7